# OTTER

## Kenneth Meadows

Illustrations by Jo Donegan

**DORLING KINDERSLEY**
LONDON • NEW YORK • SYDNEY • MOSCOW

# A DORLING KINDERSLEY BOOK

*Managing editor*: Jonathan Metcalf
*Managing art editor*: Peter Cross
*Production manager*: Michelle Thomas

The Little Library of Earth Medicine was
produced, edited and designed by
GLS Editorial and Design
Garden Studios, 11-15 Betterton Street
London WC2H 9BP

GLS Editorial and Design
*Editorial director*: Jane Laing
*Design director*: Ruth Shane
*Project designer*: Luke Herriott
*Editors*: Claire Calman, Terry Burrows, Victoria Sorzano

*Additional illustrations*: Roy Flooks 16, 17, 31; John Lawrence 38
*Special photography*: Mark Hamilton
*Picture credits*: American Natural History Museum 8-9, 12, 14-15, 32

First published in Great Britain in 1998
by Dorling Kindersley Limited
9 Henrietta Street, London WC2E 8PS

2 4 6 8 10 9 7 5 3 1

A CIP catalogue record for this book is available from the British Library

UK ISBN 0 7513 0524 3   AUSTRALIAN ISBN 1 86466 041 4

Reproduced by Kestrel Digital Colour Ltd, Chelmsford, Essex
Printed and bound in Hong Kong by Imago

# CONTENTS

## OTTER MEDICINE 25

# INTRODUCING
# EARTH MEDICINE

### TO NATIVE AMERICANS, MEDICINE IS NOT AN EXTERNAL SUBSTANCE BUT AN INNER POWER THAT IS FOUND IN BOTH NATURE AND OURSELVES.

**E**arth Medicine is a unique method of personality profiling that draws on Native American understanding of the Universe, and on the principles embodied in sacred Medicine Wheels.

Native Americans believed that spirit, although invisible, permeated Nature, so that everything in Nature was sacred. Animals were perceived as acting as

messengers of spirit. They also appeared in waking dreams to impart power known as "medicine". The recipients of such dreams honoured the animal species that appeared to them by rendering their images on ceremonial and everyday artefacts.

### NATURE WITHIN SELF

Native American shamans – tribal wisemen – recognized similarities between the natural forces prevalent during the seasons and the characteristics of those born

#### Shaman's rattle
*Shamans used rattles to connect with their inner spirit. This is a Tlingit shaman's wooden rattle.*

### "Spirit has provided you with an opportunity to study in Nature's university." *Stoney teaching*

during corresponding times of the year. They also noted how personality is affected by the four phases of the Moon – at birth and throughout life – and by the continual alternation of energy flow, from active to passive. This view is encapsulated in Earth Medicine, which helps you to recognize how the dynamics of Nature function within you and how the potential strengths you were born with can be developed.

**Animal ornament**

*To the Anasazi, who carved this ornament from jet, the frog symbolized adaptability.*

## MEDICINE WHEELS

Native American cultural traditions embrace a variety of circular symbolic images and objects. These sacred hoops have become known as Medicine Wheels, due to their similarity to the spoked wheels of the wagons that carried settlers into the heartlands of once-Native American territory. Each Medicine Wheel showed how different objects or qualities related to one another within the context of a greater whole, and how different forces and energies moved within it.

One Medicine Wheel might be regarded as the master wheel because it indicated balance within Nature and the most effective way of achieving harmony with the Universe and ourselves. It is upon this master Medicine Wheel (see pp.10–11) that Earth Medicine is structured.

**Feast dish**

*Stylized bear carvings adorn this Tlingit feast dish. To the American Indian, the bear symbolizes strength and self-sufficiency.*

# THE MEDICINE WHEEL

The outer Wheel is divided into twelve birth times, each of which has its own animal totem, and stone, tree, and colour affinities. At the hub of the Wheel, surrounded by representations of Elements, Directions, and energy flow, is the Wakan-Tanka — symbol of invisible energies coming into physical reality.

**Season of birth**
Each of the twelve segments relates to a specific time of year (see pp.12–13).

**Wakan-Tanka**
The powerful symbol used by some Native Americans to denote energy coming into form (see p.24).

NORTH: WINTER

WOLF

OTTER

GOOSE

OWL

SNAKE

WEST: AUTUMN

CROW

**Stone affinity**
Each birth time has a particular stone associated with it (see pp.14–15).

**Tree affinity**
Each birth time is connected to a type of tree (see pp.14–15).

**Birth totem**
An animal totem represents each birth time (see pp.16–17).

**Directional totem**
One of four cardinal Directions exerts an influence on each birth time (see pp.18–19).

**Principal Element**
Each birth time is fundamentally influenced by one of the four Elements (see pp.20–21).

**Energy flow**
Energy alternates between active and receptive with each birth time (see p.24).

**Elemental Aspect**
Each birth time has its own Elemental Aspect (see pp.20–21).

FALCON

BEAVER

DEER

DEER

EAST: SPRING

WOODPECKER

SALMON

BROWN BEAR

SOUTH: SUMMER

# THE TWELVE
# BIRTH TIMES

## THE STRUCTURE OF THE MEDICINE WHEEL IS BASED UPON THE SEASONS TO REFLECT THE POWERFUL INFLUENCE OF NATURE ON HUMAN PERSONALITY.

The Medicine Wheel classifies human nature into twelve personality types, each corresponding to the characteristics of Nature at a particular time of the year. It is designed to act as a kind of map to help you discover your strengths and weaknesses, your inner drives and instinctive behaviours, and your true potential.

The four seasons form the basis of the Wheel's structure, with the Summer and Winter solstices and the Spring and Autumn equinoxes marking each season's passing. In Earth Medicine,

each season is a metaphor for a stage of human growth and development. Spring is likened to infancy and the newness of life; and Summer to the exuberance of youth and of rapid development. Autumn represents the fulfilment that mature adulthood brings, while Winter symbolizes the accumulated wisdom that can be drawn upon in later life.

Each seasonal quarter of the Wheel is further divided into three periods, making twelve time segments altogether. The time of your birth determines the direction from which

### Seasonal rites

*Performers at the Iroquois mid-Winter ceremony wore masks made of braided maize husks. They danced to attune themselves to energies that would ensure a good harvest.*

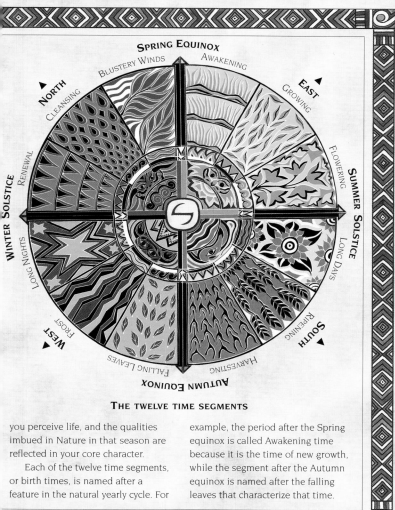

SPRING EQUINOX

AWAKENING

BLUSTERY WINDS

NORTH

EAST

CLEANSING

GROWING

RENEWAL

WINTER SOLSTICE

SUMMER SOLSTICE

FLOWERING

LONG NIGHTS

LONG DAYS

FROST

WEST

SOUTH

RIPENING

FALLING LEAVES

HARVESTING

AUTUMN EQUINOX

## THE TWELVE TIME SEGMENTS

you perceive life, and the qualities imbued in Nature in that season are reflected in your core character.

Each of the twelve time segments, or birth times, is named after a feature in the natural yearly cycle. For

example, the period after the Spring equinox is called Awakening time because it is the time of new growth, while the segment after the Autumn equinox is named after the falling leaves that characterize that time.

# THE SIGNIFICANCE OF
## TOTEMS

NATIVE AMERICANS BELIEVED THAT TOTEMS — ANIMAL SYMBOLS — REPRESENTED ESSENTIAL TRUTHS AND ACTED AS CONNECTIONS TO NATURAL POWERS.

A totem is an animal or natural object adopted as an emblem to typify certain distinctive qualities. Native Americans regarded animals, whose behaviour is predictable, as particularly useful guides to categorizing human patterns of behaviour.

A totem mirrors aspects of your nature and unlocks the intuitive knowledge that lies beyond the reasoning capacity of the intellect. It may take the form of a carving or moulding, a pictorial image, or a token of fur, feather, bone, tooth, or claw. Its presence serves as an immediate link with the energies it represents. A totem is therefore more effective than a glyph or symbol as an aid to comprehending non-physical powers and formative forces.

### PRIMARY TOTEMS
In Earth Medicine you have three primary totems: a birth totem, a Directional totem, and an Elemental totem. Your *birth totem* is the embodiment of core characteristics that correspond with the dominant aspects of Nature during your birth time.

#### Symbol of strength
*The handle of this Tlingit knife is carved with a raven and a bear head, symbols of insight and inner strength.*

All twelve birth totems, each relating to a birth time, are described on pp.16–17.

Your *Directional totem* aligns you with your inner senses, which direct the main thrust of your endeavours. Each of the four seasons on the Wheel is compatible with one of the four Directions, and each of the Directions is represented by a totem. For example, Spring is associated with the East, where the sun rises, and signifies seeing things in new ways; its totem is the Eagle. The four

**Prize totem**

*A chief or warrior of the Fox tribe affirmed his rank with this bear claw necklace.*

Directional totems are explained on pp.18–19.

Your *Elemental totem* relates to your instinctive behaviours. The qualities of the four Elements – Fire, Water, Earth, and Air – and their totems are introduced on pp.20–21.

## THREE AFFINITIES

Each birth time also has an affinity with a tree, a stone, and a colour (see pp.36–41). These three affinities have qualities that can strengthen you during challenging times.

*"If a man is to succeed, he must be governed not by his inclination, but by an understanding of the ways of animals..."* Teton Sioux teaching

# THE TWELVE
# BIRTH TOTEMS

THE TWELVE BIRTH TIMES ARE REPRESENTED BY TOTEMS,
EACH ONE AN ANIMAL THAT BEST EXPRESSES THE
QUALITIES INHERENT IN THAT BIRTH TIME.

**E**arth Medicine associates an animal totem with each birth time (the two sets of dates below reflect the difference in season between the northern and southern hemispheres). These animals help to connect you to the powers and abilities that they represent. For an in-depth study of the Otter birth totem, see pp.28–29.

## FALCON
**21 March–19 April (N. Hem)**
**22 Sept–22 Oct (S. Hem)**
Falcons are full of initiative, but often rush in to make decisions they may later regret. Lively and extroverted, they have enthusiasm for new experiences but can sometimes lack persistence.

## DEER
**21 May–20 June (N. Hem)**
**23 Nov–21 Dec (S. Hem)**
Deer are willing to sacrifice the old for the new. They loathe routine, thriving on variety and challenges. They have a wild side, often leaping from one situation or relationship into another without reflection.

## BEAVER
**20 April–20 May (N. Hem)**
**23 Oct–22 Nov (S. Hem)**
Practical and steady, Beavers have a capacity for perseverance. Good homemakers, they are warm and affectionate but need harmony and peace to avoid becoming irritable. They have a keen aesthetic sense.

## WOODPECKER
**21 June–21 July (N. Hem)**
**22 Dec–19 Jan (S. Hem)**
Emotional and sensitive, Woodpeckers are warm to those closest to them, and willing to sacrifice their needs for those of their loved ones. They have lively imaginations but can be worriers.

## SALMON
**22 July–21 August (N. Hem)**
**20 Jan–18 Feb (S. Hem)**

Enthusiastic and self-confident, Salmon people enjoy running things. They are uncompromising and forceful, and can occasionally seem a little arrogant or self-important. They are easily hurt by neglect.

## BROWN BEAR
**22 August–21 Sept (N. Hem)**
**19 Feb–20 March (S. Hem)**

Brown Bears are hardworking, practical, and self-reliant. They do not like change, preferring to stick to what is familiar. They have a flair for fixing things, are good-natured, and make good friends.

## CROW
**22 Sept–22 Oct (N. Hem)**
**21 March–19 April (S. Hem)**

Crows dislike solitude and feel most comfortable in company. Although usually pleasant and good-natured, they can be strongly influenced by negative atmospheres, becoming gloomy and prickly.

## SNAKE
**23 Oct–22 Nov (N. Hem)**
**20 April–20 May (S. Hem)**

Snakes are secretive and mysterious, hiding their feelings beneath a cool exterior. Adaptable, determined, and imaginative, they are capable of bouncing back from tough situations encountered in life.

## OWL
**23 Nov–21 Dec (N. Hem)**
**21 May–20 June (S. Hem)**

Owls need freedom of expression. They are lively, self-reliant, and have an eye for detail. Inquisitive and adaptable, they have a tendency to overextend themselves. Owls are often physically courageous.

## GOOSE
**22 Dec–19 Jan (N. Hem)**
**21 June–21 July (S. Hem)**

Goose people are far-sighted idealists who are willing to explore the unknown. They approach life with enthusiasm, determined to fulfil their dreams. They are perfectionists, and can appear unduly serious.

## OTTER
**20 Jan–18 Feb (N. Hem)**
**22 July–21 August (S. Hem)**

Otters are friendly, lively, and perceptive. They feel inhibited by too many rules and regulations, which often makes them appear eccentric. They like cleanliness and order, and have original minds.

## WOLF
**19 Feb–20 March (N. Hem)**
**22 August–21 Sept (S. Hem)**

Wolves are sensitive, artistic, and intuitive – people to whom others turn for help. They value freedom and their own space, and are easily affected by others. They are philosophical, trusting, and genuine.

# THE INFLUENCE OF THE
# DIRECTIONS

ALSO KNOWN BY NATIVE AMERICANS AS THE FOUR
WINDS, THE INFLUENCE OF THE FOUR DIRECTIONS IS
EXPERIENCED THROUGH YOUR INNER SENSES.

Regarded as the "keepers" or "caretakers" of the Universe, the four Directions or alignments were also referred to by Native Americans as the four Winds because their presence was felt rather than seen.

## DIRECTIONAL TOTEMS

In Earth Medicine, each Direction or Wind is associated with a season and a time of day. Thus the Winter birth times – Renewal time, Cleansing time, and Blustery Winds time –

all fall within the North Direction, and night. The Direction to which your birth time belongs influences the nature of your inner senses.

The East Direction is associated with illumination. Its totem is the Eagle – a bird that soars close to the Sun and can see clearly from height. The South is the Direction of Summer and the afternoon. It signifies growth and fruition, fluidity, and emotions. Its totem, the Mouse, symbolizes productivity, feelings, and an ability to perceive detail.

*"Remember...the circle of the sky, the stars, the super-natural Winds breathing night and day...the four Directions."* Pawnee teaching

**SPRING EQUINOX**

NORTH

EAST

BUFFALO

EAGLE

WINTER SOLSTICE

SUMMER SOLSTICE

### The four Directions

*Each Direction is associated with a season and a time of day, and also with a principal function: the East with determining, the South with giving, the West with holding, and the North with receiving.*

GRIZZLY BEAR

MOUSE

WEST

SOUTH

**AUTUMN EQUINOX**

The West is the Direction of Autumn and the evening. It signifies transformation – from day to night, from Summer to Winter – and the qualities of introspection and conservation. Its totem is the Grizzly Bear, which represents strength drawn from within. The North is the Direction of Winter and the night, and is associated with the mind and its sustenance – knowledge. Its totem is the Buffalo, an animal that was honoured by Native Americans as the great material "provider".

# THE INFLUENCE OF THE ELEMENTS

THE FOUR ELEMENTS — AIR, FIRE, WATER, AND EARTH —
PERVADE EVERYTHING AND INDICATE THE NATURE OF
MOVEMENT AND THE ESSENCE OF WHO YOU ARE.

lements are intangible qualities
that describe the essential state
or character of all things. In
Earth Medicine, the four Elements are
allied with four fundamental modes
of activity and are associated with
different aspects of the self. Air
expresses free movement in all
directions; it is related to the
mind and to thinking. Fire
indicates expansive
motion; it is linked with
the spirit and with
intuition. Water
signifies fluidity; it

**Elemental profile**
*The Elemental config-
uration of Otter is Air of
Air. Air is both the
Principal Element and
the Elemental Aspect.*

WATER

AIR

EARTH

FIRE

AIR

EARTH

has associations with the soul and the emotions. Earth symbolizes stability; it is related to the physical body and the sensations.

## ELEMENTAL DISTRIBUTION

On the Medicine Wheel one Element is associated with each of the four Directions – Fire in the East, Earth in the West, Air in the North, and Water in the South. These are known as the Principal Elements.

The four Elements also have an individual association with each of the twelve birth times – known as the Elemental Aspects. They follow a cyclical sequence around the Wheel based on the action of the Sun (Fire) on the Earth, producing atmosphere (Air) and condensation (Water).

The three birth times that share an Elemental Aspect belong to the same Elemental family or "clan", with a totem that gives insight into its key characteristics. Otter people belong to the Butterfly clan (see pp.34–35).

## ELEMENTAL EMPHASIS

For each birth time, the qualities of the Elemental Aspect usually predominate over those of the Principal Element, although both are present to give a specific configuration, such as Fire of Earth (for Otter's, see pp.34–35). For Falcon, Woodpecker, and Otter, the Principal Element and the Elemental Aspect are identical (for example, Air of Air), so people of these totems tend to express that Element intensely.

FIRE

EARTH

AIR

WATER

# THE INFLUENCE OF THE MOON

THE WAXING AND WANING OF THE MOON DURING ITS
FOUR PHASES HAS A CRUCIAL INFLUENCE ON THE
FORMATION OF PERSONALITY AND HUMAN ENDEAVOUR.

Native Americans regarded the Sun and Moon as indicators respectively of the active and receptive energies inherent in Nature (see p.24), as well as the measurers of time. They associated solar influences with conscious activity and the exercise of reason and the will, and lunar influences with subconscious activity and the emotional and intuitive aspects of human nature.

**The Waxing Moon**

*This phase lasts for approximately eleven days. It is a time of growth and therefore ideal for developing new ideas and concentrating your efforts into new projects.*

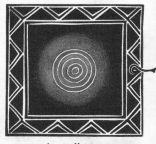

**The Full Moon**

*Lasting about three days, this is when lunar power is at its height. It is therefore a good time for completing what was developed during the Waxing Moon.*

# THE FOUR PHASES

There are four phases in the twenty-nine-day lunar cycle, each one an expression of energy reflecting a particular mode of activity. They can be likened to the phases of growth of a flowering plant through the seasons: the emergence of buds (Waxing Moon), the bursting of flowers (Full Moon), the falling away of flowers (Waning Moon), and the germination of seeds (Dark Moon). The influence of each phase can be felt in two ways: in the formation of personality and in day-to-day life.

The energy expressed by the phase of the Moon at the time of your birth has a strong influence on personality. For instance, someone born during the Dark Moon is likely to be inward-looking, whilst a person born during the Full Moon may be more expressive. Someone born during a Waxing Moon is likely to have an outgoing nature, whilst a person born during a Waning Moon may be reserved. Consult a set of Moon tables to discover the phase the Moon was in on *your* birthday.

In your day-to-day life, the benefits of coming into harmony with the Moon's energies are considerable. Experience the energy of the four phases by consciously working with them. A Native American approach is described below.

**The Waning Moon**

*A time for making changes, this phase lasts for an average of eleven days. Use it to improve and modify, and to dispose of what is no longer needed or wanted.*

**The Dark Moon**

*The Moon disappears from the sky for around four days. This is a time for contemplation of what has been achieved, and for germinating the seeds for the new.*

# THE INFLUENCE OF
# ENERGY FLOW

## THE MEDICINE WHEEL REFLECTS THE PERFECT BALANCE OF THE COMPLEMENTARY ACTIVE AND RECEPTIVE ENERGIES THAT CO-EXIST IN NATURE.

Energy flows through Nature in two complementary ways, which can be expressed in terms of active and receptive, or male and female. The active energy principle is linked with the Elements of Fire and Air, and the receptive principle with Water and Earth.

Each of the twelve birth times has an active or receptive energy related to its Elemental Aspect. Travelling around the Wheel, the two energies alternate with each birth time, resulting in an equal balance of active and receptive energies, as in Nature.

Active energy is associated with the Sun and conscious activity. Those whose birth times take this principle prefer to pursue experience. They are conceptual,

energetic, outgoing, practical, and analytical. Receptive energy is associated with the Moon and subconscious activity. Those whose birth times take this principle prefer to attract experience. They are intuitive, reflective, conserving, emotional, and nurturing.

## THE WAKAN-TANKA

At the heart of the Wheel lies an S-shape within a circle, the symbol of the life-giving source of everything that comes into physical existence – seemingly out of nothing. Named by the Plains Indians as Wakan-Tanka (Great Power), it can also be perceived as energy coming into form and form reverting to energy in the unending continuity of life.

# OTTER
# MEDICINE

### YOUR IN-DEPTH
### PERSONALITY PROFILE

# SEASON OF BIRTH
# CLEANSING TIME

## THE INVIGORATING NATURE OF WINTER REACHES ITS PEAK IN THE SECOND BIRTH TIME OF THE SEASON, LENDING THOSE BORN THEN ENTHUSIASM AND IDEALISM.

C leansing time is one of the twelve birth times, the fundamental division of the year into twelve seasonal segments (see pp.12–13). As the middle period of the Winter cycle, it is the time of year when the air is invigorating and the power of the Sun is growing perceptibly, causing a quickening to take place beneath the Earth's surface in preparation for new life.

### INFLUENCE OF NATURE

The qualities and characteristics imbued in Nature at this time form the basis of your own nature. So, just

as the Earth is preparing for the new growth of Spring, so, if you were born during Cleansing time, you have a strong need to plan ahead and a keen desire to organize both your own life and that of others. You also possess an innovative and lively mind, together with an outgoing, independent nature and a dynamic temperament that fully matches the fresh, stimulating winds of the season.

Many Native Americans celebrated the quickening of Nature in a ceremony called the Give-Away, which took place half-way through this period. It was a purification festival, mirrored in many other ancient cultures, in which participants symbolically let go of what was no longer needed and banished ill feelings, petty fears, jealousies, and bad habits. Each was represented by a stick or grain, which was cast into the fire where it was consumed.

## STAGE OF LIFE

This time of year might be compared to the maturity of the later years in life. In human development terms, it is a period in which a strong sense of independence and well-formed set of moral values is apparent. It is a time of self-assurance in which outmoded rules and regulations and unethical behaviour are abhorred, and a keen desire is felt to serve others by reforming society to achieve a greater equality of opportunity and justice, and freedom from prejudice.

## ACHIEVE YOUR POTENTIAL

You are an idealist and original thinker who seeks to improve the quality of life for everyone, and to conserve the beauty of the Earth.

**Nature's energy**

*Nature continues its austere phase in this, the middle cycle of Winter. The sharp, penetrating winds combine with the growing strength of the Sun to cleanse and stimulate the barren Earth in preparation for Spring.*

However, although many will admire your altruistic inventiveness, bear in mind that not all your ideas are feasible, and try not to become too despondent if some are rejected out of hand. Remember, you will never be short of an idea or a cause.

You are a natural organizer of people and activities but in order for your lively and analytical mind to operate efficiently, it is essential that you maintain an orderly, tidy environment both at home and at work.

*"Life is a circle from childhood to childhood; so it is with everything where power moves."* **Black Elk teaching**

# BIRTH TOTEM
# THE OTTER

### THE ESSENTIAL NATURE AND CHARACTERISTIC BEHAVIOUR OF THE OTTER EXPRESSES THE PERSONALITY TYPE OF THOSE BORN DURING CLEANSING TIME.

L ike the otter, people born during Cleansing time are constructive, friendly, adaptable, and inventive. If you were born at this time you have a lively, analytical, tolerant, and reforming nature that thrives in a free-thinking yet orderly environment.

Independent and sociable, you are a broad-minded and original thinker, with an analytical and inquisitive mind, and a talent for organization. Creative and dynamic, you are full of unusual ideas, and do not hesitate to try them out if at all feasible.

Individualistic and freedom-loving, you are also concerned for the well-being of others. Your humanitarian instincts and reforming zeal means that you are drawn to charitable activities.

## HEALTH MATTERS

An interest in alternative therapies, healthy eating, and regular exercise combine to keep you in good shape physically. Your most vulnerable area is the circulatory system, and in later life you may suffer from varicose veins and hardening of the arteries.

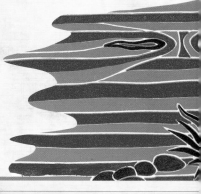

**Otter power**
*Self-assured and playful, the otter
also expresses the adaptable aspect of
the reforming people born at this time.*

# THE OTTER AND
# RELATIONSHIPS

FRIENDLY AND LIVELY, OTTER PEOPLE ARE OFTEN VERY
POPULAR. THEY MAKE GOOD-TEMPERED AND ADAPTABLE
PARTNERS BUT MAY FEEL RESTRICTED BY COMMITMENT.

**P**layful and inquisitive, Otter people, like their totem animal, are usually fun to be around. If your birth totem is Otter, your inventiveness and originality make you a stimulating companion, while your consideration for others means you are a valued friend. However, your impulsiveness and unpredictable behaviour are unsettling for some people, and your irreverence for rules and conventions can make you awkward, especially at work or on joint projects of any kind.

## LOVING RELATIONSHIPS

Although they are sociable and considerate, Otter people prize their freedom and prefer to be slightly detached. Broad-minded male Otter may be slow to settle down, while female Otter is tender but may hide her emotions. Both can be exciting lovers, but their lack of deep feelings may make for an empty love life.

When problems arise, it is often due to your restless nature, which may make your partner feel insecure. Also, your strong self-reliance and need for freedom may leave your partner feeling redundant. Try to show your feelings a little more.

## COPING WITH OTTER

Otter people are mentally agile and easily bored, so beware of waffling if you want to hold their attention. They tend to leap from one idea to another, which can frustrate progress; keep them entertained and you will help them stay focused. If you try to tie them down with too many rules, they will almost certainly rebel, so give them plenty of space.

# OTTER IN LOVE

**Otter with Falcon** If this pair can match their love life with their mental affinity, they can have a stimulating and satisfying relationship.

**Otter with Beaver** Although this might start out as a sensual relationship, these two are likely to be at odds in other areas of their lives.

**Otter with Deer** Both have vibrant and affable personalities so they should bond well together.

**Otter with Woodpecker** Life with Woodpecker may be tricky after a passionate start, especially when Otter's unconventional behaviour unsettles Woodpecker.

**Otter with Salmon** Not an easy relationship but each has the capacity to smooth out their differences.

**Otter with Brown Bear** Their love life may not move mountains, but this pair has much in common to create a lasting partnership.

**Otter with Crow** Intimacy comes easily to this pair, but Crow might find Otter's erratic behaviour trying.

**Otter with Snake** A match that needs compassion and consideration to be long-lasting – but both may be too stubborn to compromise.

**Otter with Owl** They may start out as friends but this can develop into a spirited and romantic relationship.

**Otter with Goose** While there may be sexual sparks, this may not be an easy alliance or a long-term prospect unless they can be patient with one another.

**Otter with Otter** These two believe love depends on friendship; life together may be short on passion, but they have a mutual ease that should be long-lasting.

**Otter with Wolf** Otter may be too blunt and abrasive to give sensitive Wolf the gentle affection he or she craves.

# DIRECTIONAL TOTEM
# THE BUFFALO

## THE BUFFALO SYMBOLIZES THE INFLUENCE OF THE NORTH ON OTTER PEOPLE, WHOSE MENTAL AGILITY DRIVES THEIR RESTLESS BEHAVIOUR.

R enewal time, Cleansing time, and Blustery Winds time all fall within the quarter of the Medicine Wheel associated with the North Direction or Wind.

The North is aligned with Winter and with night, and it is therefore associated with patience, the hidden energy that lies beneath the surface, purity, and renewal. It is likened to the preparation for new life and new ideas – the reflective stillness that precedes rebirth and the time of rapid growth. The power of the North's influence is primarily with the mind and wisdom, and its principal function is the power of sustenance. It takes as its totem the revered and life-sustaining buffalo.

**Buffalo skull**
*This Blackfeet-painted buffalo skull represents the buffalo, which is associated with sustenance of mind and body.*

The specific influence of the North on Otter people is on the importance of silence and listening, and of allowing yourself respite from endless activity. The power of the North is that of new life, which needs rest before it can begin to grow. It is also associated with the capacity to restore inner strength.

## BUFFALO CHARACTERISTICS
Of all animals, the buffalo was most revered by Native Americans because many tribes depended on it for their survival. Every part of it was used – its meat for food, its hide for clothing

## Spirit of the North

*The power of the North is hidden, like seeds dormant in Winter waiting to burst into new life; the Buffalo totem signifies the ability to give entirely of oneself.*

and shelter, even its bones to make tools and implements – so it was said to symbolize the spirit that gives completely of itself. It also represents applied intelligence.

If your Directional totem is Buffalo, you are likely to have a clear mind, a quiet wisdom, and the power of renewing your energies from your own inner resources.

# ELEMENTAL TOTEM
# THE BUTTERFLY

LIKE THE BUTTERFLY, WHICH FLITS FROM PLACE TO
PLACE, OTTER PEOPLE'S RESTLESS TEMPERAMENT
REQUIRES VARIETY AND FREEDOM TO MANOEUVRE.

The Elemental Aspect of Otter people is Air. They share this Aspect with Deer and Crow people, who all therefore belong to the same Elemental family or "clan" (see pp.20–21 for an introduction to the influence of the Elements).

## THE BUTTERFLY CLAN

Each Elemental clan has a totem to provide insight into its essential characteristics. The totem of the Elemental clan of Air is Butterfly, which symbolizes a quick, lively, restless, and changeable nature.

The butterfly flits here and there, seeking variety, and settling only where the atmosphere is harmonious.

**Free to change**
*The butterfly symbolizes the fundamental quality of the Element of Air: free movement.*

So if you belong to this clan you will have a lively personality and be constantly on the move – physically, mentally, and emotionally.

Quick-witted, thoughtful, and imaginative, you are full of ideas, which you are keen to communicate to others. You dislike being restricted either physically or mentally. You are quick and impatient, and crave stimulation and plenty of opportunity to express yourself.

## Air of Air

*The Air of Air influence generates mental activity and good communication skills.*

You tend to leap from one fresh venture to another and dissipate your energies, driven by the untempered urge to change that is inherent in the Air of Air configuration. So it is that you sometimes find yourself wandering off-course before you have attained your goals, leaving you feeling empty and unfulfilled.

At times like these, or when you are feeling low or lacking in energy, try the following revitalizing exercise. Find a quiet spot outside, away from the polluting effects of traffic and the activities of others, and, for several minutes, breathe slowly and deeply.

With each in-breath, acknowledge that you are drawing into yourself the energizing power of the life-force, which is being absorbed by every cell of your being, revitalizing and refreshing your whole body.

## ELEMENTAL PROFILE

For Otter people, your predominant Elemental Aspect of changeable Air is strengthened and focused by the qualities of your Principal Element – which is also Air. Consequently, if you were born at this time you are likely to exhibit mental agility and creativity, along with the power to communicate, which is bent on pioneering change and translating creative thought into tangible reality.

# STONE AFFINITY
# TURQUOISE

## BY USING THE GEMSTONE WITH WHICH YOUR OWN ESSENCE RESONATES, YOU CAN TAP INTO THE POWER OF THE EARTH ITSELF AND AWAKEN YOUR INNER STRENGTHS.

Gemstones are minerals that are formed within the Earth itself in an exceedingly slow but continuous process. Native Americans valued them not only for their beauty but also for being literally part of the Earth, and therefore possessing part of its life-force. They regarded gemstones as being "alive" – channellers of energy that could be used in many ways: to heal, to protect, or for meditation.

Every gemstone has a different energy or vibration. On the Medicine Wheel, a stone is associated with each birth time, the energy of which

**Polished turquoise**
*Turquoise was known as "the stone of the sky" and it has associations with the mystical realm. It was prized for the intensity of its colour.*

resonates with the essence of those born during that time. Because of this energy affiliation, your stone can help bring you into harmony with the Earth and create balance within yourself. It can enhance and develop your good qualities and endow you with the abilities you need.

## ENERGY RESONANCE

Otter people have an affinity with turquoise, a sky-blue or green-blue stone that has been mined for over 3,000 years. Turquoise is regarded as highly sensitive and is said to change colour if its wearer is unwell or in

# ACTIVATE YOUR GEMSTONE

Obtain a piece of turquoise and cleanse it by holding it under cold running water. Allow it to dry naturally, then, holding the stone with both hands, bring it up to your mouth and blow into it sharply and hard three or four times in order to impregnate it with your breath. Next, hold it firmly in one hand and silently welcome it into your life as a friend and helper.

When you are stressed or finding it hard to express yourself well, use the turquoise to help you meditate. Find a quiet spot to sit, keep the soles of your feet on the floor, and hold the stone in the hollow of your throat with your right hand. Focus on the stone; let it disperse any negativity clouding your thoughts and lead you towards clarity. Listen for the still, quiet voice of your inner self.

danger. Native Americans wore it as a protection against injury, especially broken bones, and valued it as a healing stone which strengthened the body and relieved any disorder.

If your birth totem is Otter, you will find turquoise a valuable aid in guarding against

**Turquoise power**
*To benefit most from its effect, wear turquoise and keep a stone in a prominent place in your home to promote peace.*

emotional disturbance, helping you retain your balance under pressure. Symbolically linking sky and Earth – spiritual and practical – turquoise helps you balance these two aspects of life. It is also thought to bring clarity, so aids oral and written communication.

**"The outline of the stone is round; the power of the stone is endless."** Lakota Sioux teaching

# TREE AFFINITY
## ASH

GAIN A DEEPER UNDERSTANDING OF YOUR OWN NATURE
AND AWAKEN POWERS LYING DORMANT WITHIN YOU BY
RESPECTING AND CONNECTING WITH YOUR AFFINITY TREE.

Trees have an important part to play in the protection of Nature's mechanisms and in the maintenance of the Earth's atmospheric balance, which is essential for the survival of the human race.

Native Americans referred to trees as "Standing People" because they stand firm, obtaining strength from their connection with the Earth. They therefore teach us the importance of being grounded, whilst at the same time listening to, and reaching for, our higher aspirations. When respected as living beings, trees can provide insight into the workings of Nature and our own inner selves.

On the Medicine Wheel, each birth time is associated with a particular kind of tree, the basic qualities of which complement the nature of those born during that time. Otter people have an affinity with the ash. Prized for its qualities of toughness and elasticity, the timber of the ash has as many uses as the inventive and dynamic Otter has schemes. This tall tree has deep roots, giving its lofty canopy a

# CONNECT WITH YOUR TREE

Appreciate the beauty of your affinity tree and study its nature carefully, for it has an affinity with your own nature.

The ash is a tall and stately tree with deep roots, thick branches, and winged seed capsules – ash "keys" – carried far by the wind. Its toughness and elasticity have long made it valued for joists and furniture, bows and spears, tools, ladders, and carts.

Try the following exercise when you need to revitalize your inner strength. Stand beside your affinity tree. Place the palms of your hands on its trunk and rest your forehead on the backs of your hands. Inhale slowly and experience energy from the tree's roots flow through your body. If easily available, obtain a cutting or twig from your affinity tree to keep as a totem or helper.

firm foundation. Otter people are visionaries and reformers, but some of their ideas lack practicality. Consequently, they need to learn how to keep their ideas grounded in reality. Otter people can tap into the ash's strong link with the earth by connecting with their tree (see panel above).

## FLEXIBLE YET FIRM

If your birth totem is Otter, you are innovative, dynamic, and good at organizing people, but you tend to

take on too many commitments so can let yourself down by leaping from one project to another.

One of the greatest challenges Otter people face is turning visions into reality. Like the ash, whose timber's flexibility is bolstered by great strength, you need endurance to achieve your goals. Draw on the energy of the ash; its resilience will help you maintain your spirits and keep your focus, and ensure that you find greater fulfilment.

*"All healing plants are given by Wakan-Tanka; therefore they are holy."* **Lakota Sioux teaching**

# COLOUR AFFINITY
# SILVER-GREY

ENHANCE YOUR POSITIVE QUALITIES BY USING THE
POWER OF YOUR AFFINITY COLOUR TO AFFECT YOUR
EMOTIONAL AND MENTAL STATES.

Each birth time has an affinity with a particular colour. This is the colour that resonates best with the energies of the people born during that time. Exposure to your affinity colour will encourage a positive emotional and mental response, while exposure to colours that clash with your affinity colour will have a negative effect on your sense of well-being.

Silver-grey resonates with Otter people. Associated with quicksilver mental agility, perception, and intuition, silver-grey is the colour of the intellect and the light of the Moon. It suggests ingenuity and inventiveness, together with concentration and clarity. The colour of honesty and trust, silver-grey

### Colour scheme

*Feel the full benefit of your colour affinity. Let a silver-grey colour theme be the thread that runs through your home, from the ornaments to the fixtures and fittings.*

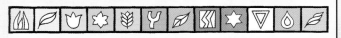

# BREATHE IN YOUR COLOUR

Take a small silver object, such as a decorative tin, and polish it so that it gleams. Place it near an open window and stand before it with your legs slightly apart, so that your weight is evenly distributed.

Focus on the colour and inhale slowly through the nose. Imagine that the air you breathe in is the colour of the object. Hold the breath for a few seconds and feel that colour filtering through your entire body, energizing every cell. Breathe out slowly. Pause, then begin the sequence again. Continue this rhythmic colour breathing for at least three or four minutes in order to experience its positive effects fully.

embodies liveliness, idealism, integrity, and the ability to stick with determination to your principles whatever the situation and whoever you are dealing with.

## COLOUR BENEFITS

Strengthen your aura and enhance your positive qualities by introducing shades of silver-grey to the interior decor of your home. Spots of colour can make all the difference. A silver motif on the curtains or wallpaper, for example, can alter the ambience of a room, or try placing a large, silver-framed mirror on the wall, or similarly framed photographs on the mantelpiece.

If you need a confidence boost, wear something that contains silver, such as a brooch, necklace, or cuff-links. Whenever your energies are low, practise the colour breathing exercise outlined above to balance your emotions, awaken your creativity, and help you to feel joyful.

*"The power of the spirit should be honoured with its colour."* Lakota Sioux teaching

# WORKING THE WHEEL
# LIFE PATH

CONSIDER YOUR BIRTH PROFILE AS A STARTING POINT IN
THE DEVELOPMENT OF YOUR CHARACTER AND THE
ACHIEVEMENT OF PERSONAL FULFILMENT.

Each of the twelve birth times is associated with a particular path of learning, or with a collection of lessons to be learned through life. By following your path of learning you will develop strengths in place of weaknesses, achieve a greater sense of harmony with the world, and discover inner peace.

## YOUR PATH OF LEARNING
For Otter people, the first lesson on your path of learning is to see your life as

a continuous road of development in which new experiences grow out of old ones, and successes emerge out of the struggles and challenges of the past. Try to look at each new experience, relationship, or job in the context of what has gone before so that you can avoid repeating previous mistakes and adapt your behaviour to suit the new circumstances. In this way you will

*"Each man's road is shown to him within his own heart. There he sees all the truths of life."* Cheyenne teaching

continue to develop as a person and maximize the chances of success in love and work in the future.

Otter people must also develop the ability to turn their visions into practical reality. Next time you have an innovative idea, analyse it carefully and break it down into its component parts. Then consider how each part might be implemented and work through the individual tasks needed to complete each one. Finally, proceed step-by-step through these tasks until you achieve the completion of your goal. Your third lesson is to develop the

courage and determination to persist with the implementation of your ideas despite disappointments and setbacks. Very little of lasting value is achieved without endeavour. Try to view each obstacle you encounter as a challenge that, once overcome, marks a milestone in the path towards your ultimate goal.

# WORKING THE WHEEL
# MEDICINE POWER

## HARNESS THE POWERS OF OTHER BIRTH TIMES TO TRANSFORM YOUR WEAKNESSES INTO STRENGTHS AND MEET THE CHALLENGES IN YOUR LIFE.

The whole spectrum of human qualities and abilities is represented on the Medicine Wheel. The totems and affinities associated with each birth time indicate the basic qualities with which those born at that time are equipped.

Study your path of learning (see pp.42–43) to identify those aspects of your personality that may need to be strengthened, then look at other birth times to discover the totems and affinities that can assist you in this task. Your Elemental profile is Air of Air (see pp.34–35), so for balance you need the stability of Earth, the adaptability of Water, and

**Complementary affinity**

*A key strength of Salmon – weak in Otter – is the determination to put ideas into practice.*

the enthusiasm of Fire. Falcon's Elemental profile is Fire of Fire, Brown Bear's is Earth of Water, and Snake's is Water of Earth, so meditate on these birth totems. In addition, you may find it useful to study the profiles of the other two members of your Elemental clan of Butterfly – Deer and Crow – to discover how the same Elemental Aspect can be expressed differently.

Also helpful is the birth totem that sits opposite yours on the Medicine Wheel, which contains qualities and characteristics that complement or enhance your own. This is known as your complementary affinity, which for Otter people is Salmon.

# ESSENTIAL STRENGTHS

Described below are the essential strengths of each birth totem. To develop a quality that is weak in yourself or that you need to meet a particular challenge, meditate upon the birth totem that contains the attribute you need. Obtain a representation of the relevant totem – a claw, tooth, or feather; a picture, ring, or model. Affirm that the power it represents is within you.

**Falcon medicine** is the power of keen observation and the ability to act decisively and energetically whenever action is required.

**Beaver medicine** is the ability to think creatively and laterally – to develop alternative ways of doing or thinking about things.

**Deer medicine** is characterized by sensitivity to the intentions of others and to that which might be detrimental to your well-being.

**Woodpecker medicine** is the ability to establish a steady rhythm throughout life and to be tenacious in protecting all that you hold dear.

**Salmon medicine** is the strength to be determined and courageous in the choice of goals you want to achieve and to have enough stamina to see a task through to the end.

**Brown Bear medicine** is the ability to be resourceful, hardworking, and dependable in times of need, and to draw on inner strength.

**Crow medicine** is the ability to transform negative or non-productive situations into positive ones and to transcend limitations.

**Snake medicine** is the talent to adapt easily to changes in circumstances and to manage transitional phases well.

**Owl medicine** is the power to see clearly during times of uncertainty and to conduct life consistently, according to long-term plans.

**Goose medicine** is the courage to do whatever might be necessary to protect your ideals and adhere to your principles in life.

**Otter medicine** is the ability to connect with your inner child, to be innovative and idealistic, and to thoroughly enjoy the ordinary tasks and routines of everyday life.

**Wolf medicine** is the courage to act according to your intuition and instincts rather than your intellect, and to be compassionate.